A Reflective Self Discovery **Workbook**

Y.O.U.R.S.

YOUR OWN UNIQUE REAL SELF

Create a BRAND of
Y.O.U.R.S.

ENGEL JONES

Editors:
Amanda Jones
Mitzy Sandy
Christian Ali
Rondel Benjamin

Publisher:
Amazel Enterprise

Book Layout Designer:
Arbëresh Dalipi

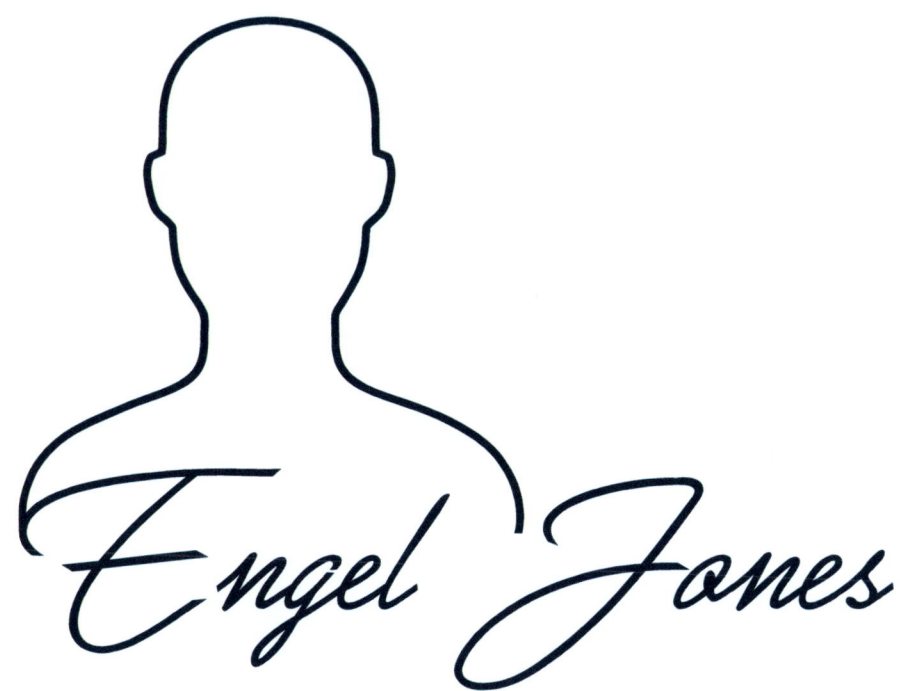

Victory
I set a goal to have 1509 conversations as part of my podcast on iTunes called "Twelve
Minute Convos w/ Engel Jones" and went for it.
I got to 1001 conversations over 3 months :)
All of this would not have been possible without my team.

My Family- who needed to be really quiet while recording and who did not have
as many conversations as they would regularly have with me.

My Business Team- Amazing Activators Francis Gil Barcial- Sound Engineer
of all #12minconvos (He has listened to me more than me :)
Ricky Policarpio - The connector. Ricky represents the conversations I needed
to have but could not. He established many important connections.
Jayson Cubao allowed us to stay stable.
Liezl Villanueva Obedencio & Irene Servano Galacio reflected our brand in the
best way possible through their creative capacity.

My Mastermind Team lead by Jamie Slingerland helped to maintain the
balance:-
Colby Parks
Gabriel Merino
Justin Parks
Paco Maldonado

My Local Trini Mastermind
Rondel Benjamin
Christian Ali

This book was designed by the very best book designer I know
Arbëresh Dalipi.

All of this started with a conversation. The power of a conversation is truly
AMAZING.

To all Thank You (with tears in my eyes as I type)

Thank You!!!!!!!!!!!!

Thank You God!!!

God is D Boss!!!

INTRODUCTION

After having 1001 conversations over a three month period, I was truly amazed by how listening to the story of others could impact one's journey of self discovery. Those stories shared were recorded and released on the airwaves via twelve minute capsules. This workbook now gives you the opportunity to search, find and scribe what is **Y.O.U.R.S.** This acronym is personalized because it's all about YOU and it's threefold in nature.

Your Own Unique Real Story unfolds as you delve into your earliest childhood memory. This being a likely influencer of your adult life, helps you develop **Your Own Unique Real Statement -** your distinctive personal statement for life. The establishment of these have proven to be pivotal to the discovery of **Your Own Unique Real Self.**
So have fun as you discover **Y.O.U.R.S.**— your personal brand.

Points to remember when using this book:

(1) Be true to yourself. Answer each question with total honesty. It is the key to discovering Your Own Unique Real Self.

(2) With your answers there are some which will be constant while there are those which may change over time. These you can revisit and reassess. A pencil or erasable pen might come in handy here.

3)When you've identified the elements which gives clarity to Your Own Unique Real Self you should highlight them so that they can be drawn upon if ever you are in a state of indecision.

4) If you require the assistance of Engel Jones to clarify the vision of Your Own Unique Real Self you can contact him at **www.twelveminuteconvos.com/coach**

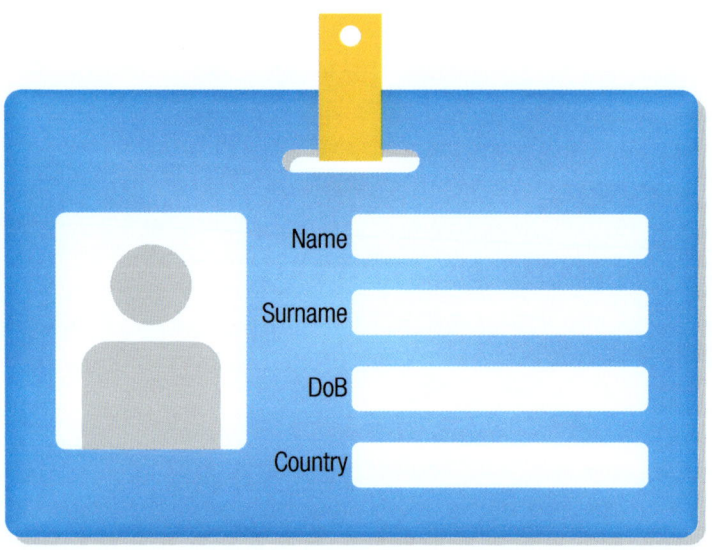

"It isn't what they call you, it's what you answer to"
- W.C Fields

My name means...

_____

_____

_____

_____

My name was given to me by...

_____

_____

_____

_____

My birth date is _____
Amazing things that happened on that date

_____

_____

_____

_____

_____

Decisive	Interactive	Stabilizing	Cautious
Problems:	People:	Pace:	Procedures:
How you tend to approach problems and makes decisions	How you tend to interact with others and share opinions	How you tend to pace things in your environment	Your preference for established protocol/ standards
High D	**High I**	**High S**	**High C**
Demanding	**Gregarious**	**Patient**	**Cautious**
Driving	Persuasive	Predictable	Perfectionist
Forceful	Inspiring	Passive	Systematic
Daring	Enthusiastic	Complacent	Careful
Determined	Sociable	Stable	Analytical
Competitive	Poised	Consistent	Orderly
Responsible	Charming	Steady	Neat
Inquisitive	Convincing	Outgoing	Balanced
Conservative	Reflective	Restless	Independent
Mild	Matter-of-fact	Active	Rebellious
Agreeable	Withdrawn	Spontaneous	Careless
Unobtrusive	**Aloof**	**Impetuous**	**Defiant**
Low D	**Low I**	**Low S**	**Low C**

"Appearance makes impressions but it's the personality
that makes an impact"
- Unknown

Circle three words that most accurately describes you.

D	**i**	**S**	**C**
Decisive	Interactive	Stable	Cautious

I tend to approach problems and makes decisions?	How you tend to interact with others and share opinions?	How you tend to pace things in your environment?	Your preference for established rules and regulations?
Demanding	Gregarious	Patient	Cautious
Driving	Persuasive	Predictable	Perfectionist
Forceful	Inspiring	Passive	Systematic
Daring	Enthusiastic	Complacent	Careful
Determined	Sociable	Stable	Analytical
Competitive	Poised	Consistent	Orderly
Responsible	Charming	Steady	Neat
Inquisitive	Convincing	Outgoing	Balanced
Conservative	Reflective	Restless	Independent
Mild	Matter-of-fact	Active	Rebellious
Agreeable	Withdrawn	Spontaneous	Careless
Unobtrusive	Aloof	Impetuous	Defiant

"Successful people use their strength by recognizing, developing, and utilizing the talents of others."
- Zig Ziglar

Y.O.U.R.S.
YOUR OWN UNIQUE REAL SELF

My Talent/Skill is...

_____

_____

_____

_____

_____

_____

I use my talent/skill in the following ways

To improve myself
_____

_____

_____

_____

To improve my family
_____

_____

_____

_____

To improve my friends
_____

_____

_____

_____

"To be a champion you have to believe
when no one else will."
- Sugar Ray Robinson

Awards/Honors/Appreciation at:

Ages 1-9

Ages 10-17

Ages 18-24

Ages 25- 50

Age 50+

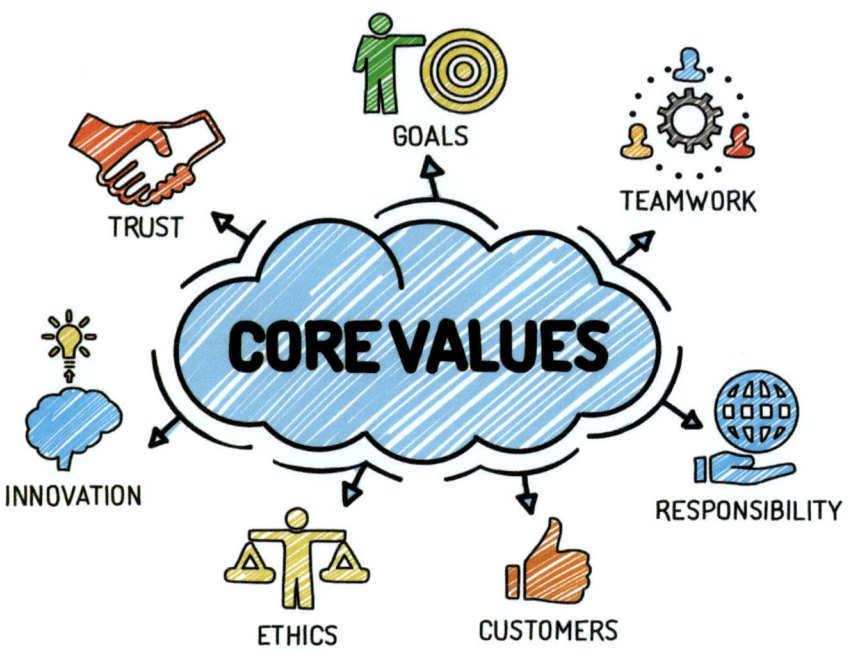

"Keep your values positive because your
values become your destiny."
- M. Ghandi

What KEY lessons have I learned from the following?

Family

_____
_____
_____
_____
_____
_____

Mentors/Teachers

_____
_____
_____
_____
_____
_____

Friends

_____
_____
_____
_____
_____
_____

"It always seems impossible until it's done."
- Nelson Mandela

My plan for using my skills:

Daily

_____
_____
_____
_____
_____
_____

Weekly

_____
_____
_____
_____
_____

Monthly

_____
_____
_____
_____
_____
_____

"Accountability breeds response-ability"
-Stephen Covey

Who from the following can help me to be accountable
with my skills?

Family (How?)

_____

_____

_____

_____

_____

Mentors/Teachers (How?)

_____

_____

_____

_____

_____

Friends (How?)

_____

_____

_____

_____

_____

_____

"We are what we repeatedly do"
-Aristotle

Additional skills I would like to have?

Caring ☐

Common sense ☐

Cooperation ☐

Curiosity ☐

Effort ☐

Flexibility ☐

Friendship ☐

Initiative ☐

Integrity ☐

Organization ☐

Patience ☐

Perseverance ☐

Problem solving ☐

Responsibility ☐

Sense of humor ☐

_____ ☐

_____ ☐

_____ ☐

"Small disciplines repeated with consistency everyday
lead to great achievments gained slowly over time"
- John C. Maxwell

In order to gain these new skills I must do/adopt the following habits:

Daily

_____

_____

_____

_____

_____

_____

Weekly

_____

_____

_____

_____

_____

_____

Monthly

_____

_____

_____

_____

_____

_____

"Continuous effort - not strength or intelligence -
is the key to unlocking our potential"
-Winston Churchill

Activities I have done consistently in the following areas
of my life are:

INTELLECTUAL

SPIRITUAL

CAREER

PHYSICAL

FINANCIAL

PERSONAL

FAMILY

"Feelings or emotions are the universal language and are to be honored. They are the authentic expression of who you are at your deepest place".
- Judith Wright

How has remaining consistent benefitted me in the following areas?

INTELLECTUAL

SPIRITUAL

CAREER

PHYSICAL

FINANCIAL

PERSONAL

FAMILY

"Memories are the architecture of our identity"
- Unknown.

My earliest or favorite childhood memory
was at the age of _____ years old

Describe this memory in detail (if possible)...

_____

_____

_____

_____

_____

_____

_____

_____

_____

_____

_____

_____

_____

_____

_____

_____

_____

_____

_____

_____

_____

"A picture is worth a thousand words,
but the memories are priceless"
- Unknown

I remember this memory clearly because at this time...

"Sometimes you will never know the true value
of a moment until it becomes a memory"
- Unknown

I interpret this memory as...

Where WORDS fail MUSIC speaks
- Hans Christian Anderson

My favorite song/songs when I was 12 years old

1) _____

2) _____

3) _____

4) _____

5) _____

Some other songs I love

1) _____

2) _____

3) _____

4) _____

5) _____

"Behind every favorite song lies an untold story"
- Unknown

These songs connect to my story in the following way…

"With time our indecisions become
decisions that life takes for us"
-Roxanna Jones

Have you chosen to share/ pass on your skills?

Check your answer

☐   ☐

"What you do is your history and
what you set in motion is your legacy".
- Leonard Sweet.

Explain:

If yes, why do you think sharing your skill is important?

_____

_____

_____

_____

_____

_____

_____

_____

_____

_____

If no, why not?

_____

_____

_____

_____

_____

_____

_____

_____

_____

"Relationships are the hallmark of the mature person".
Brian Tracy

What is your Marital Status?

Single ☐

Married ☐

Partner ☐

Separated ☐

Divorced ☐

"Life is 10% what happens to you
and 90% how you react to it"
-Charles R. Swindoll

The story of my marital status:

_____

_____

_____

_____

_____

_____

_____

_____

_____

_____

_____

_____

_____

_____

_____

_____

_____

_____

_____

_____

_____

_____

_____

_____

_____

_____

_____

_____

_____

_____

_____

"Children are the keys of paradise."
- Eric Hoffer

Do you have children?

Yes ☐   No ☐

If yes, how have children impacted your life?

_____

_____

_____

_____

_____

_____

_____

_____

If no, explain if you desire to

_____

_____

_____

_____

_____

_____

_____

_____

_____

"The greatness of a nation and its moral progress
can be judged by the way its animals are treated."
-M.Ghandi

Do you have pets?

☐ Yes ☐ No

If yes, how many?

_____
_____
_____

What type of pets?

_____
_____
_____
_____
_____
_____
_____

If no, explain why this is so

_____
_____
_____
_____
_____
_____

"It is in your moments of decision
that your destiny is shaped."
-Tony Robbins

Do I have a spiritual belief

☐ Yes   ☐ No

Who or What inspired my spiritual belief?

_____
_____
_____
_____
_____
_____
_____
_____

My Personal Testimony

_____
_____
_____
_____
_____
_____
_____
_____
_____

The language of friendship is not words but meanings."
-H.D. Thoreau

Y.O.U.R.S.
YOUR OWN UNIQUE REAL SELF

Do you have an inner circle of friends?

☐ Yes   ☐ No

If yes, describe them

_____

_____

_____

_____

_____

_____

_____

_____

_____

If no, explain why this is so

_____

_____

_____

_____

_____

_____

_____

_____

_____

"Technology is a useful servant but a dangerous master."
-Christian L. Lange

Do you watch TV for more than

3 hours a day ☐ Yes ☐ No

3 hours a week ☐ Yes ☐ No

Watching TV provides me with the following

_____

_____

_____

_____

_____

_____

_____

_____

_____

_____

_____

_____

_____

_____

_____

_____

_____

_____

_____

"The time is always right to do what is right."
-Martin Luther King, Jr.

Do you spend more than 8 hours a day on the phone and/or computer?

☐ Yes   ☐ No

My reason for this is:

_____

_____

_____

_____

_____

_____

_____

_____

_____

_____

_____

_____

_____

_____

_____

_____

_____

_____

_____

_____

Engel's example

Y.O.U.R.S
Your Own Unique Real Statement.

To create an active, sharing online community powered by warm, inspiring, authentic conversations.

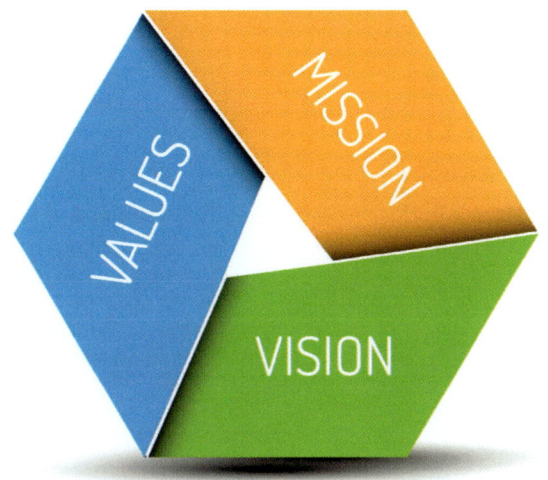

Y.O.U.R.S
Your Own Unique Real Stance.

To encourage warm conversations with people who are uniquely different but who share the similarities of an authentic, integrity driven passion to inspire the world.

Y.O.U.R.S
Your Own Unique Real Self.

Helping YOU the Entrepreneur CREATE A BRAND OF Y.O.U.R.S-Your Own Unique Real Self

Your Own Unique Real Self (Vision)

After self-reflection this is the vision I see for myself...

_____

_____

_____

How will living by this Vision impact

Me _____

_____

_____

_____

_____

My family _____

_____

_____

_____

_____

My friends: _____

_____

_____

_____

_____

Your Own Unique Real Statement (Mission)

This is a sentence that you live by.

_____

_____

_____

How will living by this statement impact

Me _____

_____

_____

_____

_____

My family _____

_____

_____

_____

_____

My friends _____

_____

_____

_____

_____

Your Own Unique Real Stance (VALUES)

These are the values that I build on.

_____

_____

_____

How will living by these values impact

Me:
_____

_____

_____

_____

_____

My family
_____

_____

_____

_____

My friends
_____

_____

_____

_____

Your Own Unique Real Story

This is my story
_____

_____

_____

_____

_____

_____

_____

_____

_____

_____

_____

_____

_____

_____

_____

_____

_____

_____

_____

_____

_____

_____

_____

Below and continuing is a list of all of the people I had a conversation with up to the point of creating this workbook.

- A.G Billig
- Aaron Walker
- Aaron Watson
- Abby Sevcik
- Ace Chapman
- Adam Franklin
- Adam Kraai
- Adam Lerner
- Adam Newman
- Adanna Austin
- Aditya Jaykumar
- Adrian Aguilar
- Adrian Havelock
- Adrian Sealey
- Adrienne Barker
- Agatha Cassidy
- Ahmed Muzammil
- Aidan Lee
- Ais Sarah
- Akosua D. Edwards
- Al Clunnie
- Albert Williams
- Alethea Fitzpatrick
- Alex Barker
- Alex Berman
- Alex Genadinik
- Alex Rodriguez
- Ali Rittenhouse
- Alicia Rodriguez
- Allie McAdam
- Allison Schaaf
- Allyson Hawkins Ward
- Alyson Garrido

- Amanda Doughty
- Amanda Heal
- Amanda Jones
- Amanda Kingsley
- Amanda Neill
- Amar Vyas
- Amber Brogly
- Amelie Chanda
- Amit Shah
- Ammeth Ruparella
- Amy Honey
- Amy Oestreicher
- Ana Hoffman
- Anastasia Button
- Andre Loubier
- Andre Waltz
- Andrea Bergin
- Andrea Hill
- Andrea Pennington
- Andrea Riggs
- Andreas Jones
- Andrew Buckwalter
- Andrew McCauley
- Andrew Schreiber
- Andrise Bass
- Andy Cumming
- Anfernee Chansamooth
- Angel Taylor
- Angela Dee
- Angela Powers
- Angus Nelson
- Anita Narayan
- Anke Hermann

- Anna Liotta
- Annabel Melnyk
- Annick Ina
- Annie Pool
- Anthony Hayes
- Anthony Lambert
- Anthony Tenaglier
- Anthony Tran
- Anthony Vaughan
- Anthony Verna
- Anthony Witt
- Antonio Crawford
- April Henheffer
- April Jones
- Arel Moodie
- Ari Meisel
- Ariana Sylvester
- Arne Giske
- Asa Leveaux
- Asha Mankowska
- Ashley Emma
- Ashley James
- Ashley Logsdon
- Audrey Rich
- Avrohom Gottheil
- Axel Howerton
- Ayesha Hilton
- Baila Lazarus
- Barry Watson
- Becky De Acetis
- Becky Erkkila
- Becky Robinson
- Beejal Parmar

- Ben Krueger
- Benjamin Newman
- Bernadette Slowey
- Bernard Kelvin Clive
- Bethel Nathan
- Betty-Ann Pilgrim
- Bhomik Saini
- Bill Caskey
- Bill Dow
- Bill Nowicki
- Bob Burg
- Bob Minhas
- Bobby Casey
- Boom Shikha
- Brad Baldridge
- Brad DeGraw
- Brad Rudher
- Bradley Morley & Greg Nicholls
- Brady Patterson
- Brandi Stephens
- Brandon Adams
- Brandon Allen
- Brandon Schaefer
- Bree Noble
- Bren Dube
- Brenda Paulous
- Brett Campbell
- Brian Basilico
- Brian Benson
- Brian King
- Brighton West
- Brodie Welch

- Brooklyn Dicent
- Bruce Van Horn
- Bruno Gama
- Bryan Weinert
- Cade Joiner
- Caden Parks
- Calvin Simpson
- Calvin Wayman
- Cami Baker
- Candice Davis
- Cara Brzezinki
- Cardiff Hall
- Carl Bischoff
- Carly Evans
- Carmen Farmer
- Carol Wain
- Carol Williams
- Carol Zurita
- Caroline Balinska
- Caroline Greene
- Caroline Southwell
- Carolyn Cole
- Caron Asgarali
- Casey Plouffe
- Casey Sullivan
- Cat Rose
- Cate Montana
- Catherine Basy
- Catherine Ewing
- Catherine Saykaly-Stevens
- Catherine Storing
- Cathy O'Dowd

- Celeste St Hill
- Chad Bostic
- Chandler Bolt
- Chantell Verma-Johnson
- Chara Watson
- Charlene Burke
- Charles Byrd
- Charlie Birch
- Chef Leo Spizzirri
- Cherie Aimee
- Cheryl Chapman
- Cheryl Major
- Cheryl Smith
- Cheval John
- Chip Lake
- Chloe Hung
- Chloe Thomas
- Chris Braaten
- Chris Drabenstott
- Chris Fern
- Chris Green
- Chris Jones
- Chris McClure
- Chris Miles
- Chris Niemeyer
- Chris O'Byrne
- Chris Pritchard
- Chris Puckett
- Chris Ripka
- Chris Ruggiero
- Chris Seiter
- Chris Sprague

76

- Christian Ali
- Christina Alexandra
- Christina Canters
- Christina Christou from Alkehela
- Christine Boyle
- Christine Mims
- Christine Powers
- Christobel Llewellyn
- Christopher Lin
- Christopher Orangeo
- Christopher Wallin
- Chrysty Lee
- Cindy Ashton
- Cindy Marvin
- Cindy Zu
- Civilla Morgan
- Claire Yanta-O'Mahoney
- Clarissa Wilson
- Clay Green
- Clayton Groves
- Coach Michael Burt
- Colby Parks
- Cole Johnson
- Cole Oliver
- Colin Ngai
- Colin Wiebe
- Colleen Keith
- Connie Ragen Green
- Corey Poirier
- Craig Wyman
- Curt Stowers
- Curtis McHale

- Damion Lupo
- Dan Hegerich
- Dan McDaniel
- Dan Morris
- Dan Simon
- Dana Pharant
- Dana Sanchez
- Dani DiPirro
- Daniel Bauer
- Daniel Bishop
- Daniel Hanzelka
- Daniel Margolin
- Daniel Maw
- Daniel Tieman
- Daniella Blechner
- Danna Pycher
- Danny Walsh
- Daphne Smith
- Darlene Waye
- Darren Carrington
- Daryl Urbanski
- Dave Bullis
- Dave Chesson
- Dave Elliott
- Dave Schneider
- Dave Visaya
- Dave Wakeman
- David Bonai
- David Jackson
- David Kosciusko
- David Ralph
- David Sandy
- Dawn Fotopulos

- Dayne Gingrich
- Deacon Hayes
- Debbie Owen
- Deidre Proctor
- Delia Athey
- Demi Karpouzos
- Denicea Hilton
- Denise Damijo
- Denise Mago
- Denise Wagstaff
- Denise Wakeman
- Dennis Washington
- Derek Loudermilk
- Derrick Kwa
- Devi Ward
- Di Riddel
- Diane Gardner
- Diego Slingerland
- Dina Eisenberg
- Divora Elishaba
- Don Dacian
- Doneane Beckcom
- Donna Barker
- Donnie Bryant
- Dooug Stewart
- Dori Staehle
- Dorottya Eva Kiss
- Doug McIssac
- Dov Baron
- Dr. Anita Jackson
- Dr. Denise Dennis
- Dr. Frederick Jones
- Dr. Lauren Noel

- Dr. Mary Jo Odom-Dull
- Dr. Phillip Carson
- Dr. Ritamarie Loscalzo
- Dr. Ulwyn Pierre
- Dr. Voice
- Duana Welch
- Dustin Heiner
- Ed Roman
- Eddy Mann
- Eddys Velasquez
- Edward Plant
- Elaine Mc Guinness
- Elayna Fernandez
- Eldyka Simpson
- Elena Rahrig
- Elias Schroons
- Elisabeth Stitl
- Elizabeth Johnston
- Elle Roetzel
- Ellen Finkelstein
- Elvisa Kovacevic
- Emillie Shoop
- Emily Chadbourne
- Emily Kiing
- Emily Merrell
- Emily Nature
- Emily Rose
- Emma Chard-Cumming
- Engelo Rumora
- Eric Eaton
- Eric Gonia
- Eric Sazer
- Erica Duran

- Erica Glessing
- Erica Gordon
- Erik Newton
- Erin Obrien
- Erin Ward
- Erlinda Vo
- Errol Fabien
- Estellita Gonzalez
- Esther Nagle
- Fabienne Raphaël
- Fateema Karim
- Frances Richards
- Francesca Gordon-Smith
- Francine Shaw
- Francis Gil Barcial
- Frank Benedetto
- Frank Bria
- Frank Cottle
- Frank Daley
- Frank Gibson
- Frank Salas
- Frans Van Liempt
- Fred Mastromarino
- Gabriel Aviles
- Gabriel Merino
- Gary Loper
- Gary Tessero
- Gaurav Mishra
- Gene Hammett
- Geoff Nicholoson
- Gerald Vinci
- Gerhard Paasche

- Gia Ganesh
- Gil Barham
- Gillian Wormley
- Gina Ryan
- Gina VanLuven
- Ginger M
- Ginny Carter
- Giovanna Capozza
- Glen Kirkpatrick
- Gloria Hass
- Gloria Kimberly
- Gloya McRae
- Gordie Bufton
- Gordon Noice
- Goro Gupta
- Grace Carter
- Graham Honeycutt
- Graham Spinks
- Greg Boudle
- Guy Daigneault
- H Cortez
- Hal Elrod
- Halelly Azulay
- Hamid Safaei
- Hani Mourra
- Hans Finzel
- Harry Duran
- Hatim Kanaaneh
- Havilland Maxwell
- Heather Ann Havenwood
- Heather Chauvin
- Heather Criswell

- Heather Ordover
- Helen Rebello
- Helena Summer
- Hilary Lauren
- Hilory Walk
- Hira Ali
- Holly Reid
- Holly Sully
- Holly Whorton
- Honoree Corder
- Ian MacMilan
- Ilka Oster
- Iman Aghay
- Inez Bracy
- Inez Ruiz
- Interviewee
- Isabel Dennis
- Isiah Fowler
- Ivan Raiklin
- Jack Dawhra
- Jackie Dinsmore
- Jackie Vandervelde
- Jacque Nagy
- Jacqui Letran
- Jacquie Johnston-Lynch
- Jaida Steele
- Jaimie Jay
- Jamea Zuberi
- James Erdt
- James Farrelly
- James Newcomb
- James Porritt

- James Wightman
- Jamie Brown
- Jamie Honey
- Jamie Slingerland
- Jamie Sullivan
- Jamila Jeffers
- Jason Freeman
- Jason Legaard
- Jason Levy
- Jason Rogers
- Jason Rosenblum
- Jay Parks
- Jean Kay
- Jean Lanoue
- Jean Leggett
- Jeanet Annoff
- Jeet Banerjee
- Jeff Desjardin
- Jeff Echols
- Jeff McMahon
- Jeff Moore
- Jeff Pierce
- Jeff Spencer
- Jeff Werner
- Jeff Williams
- Jeff Williams Jnr
- Jeffery Perry
- Jeffrey DeSocio
- Jeffrey Kramer
- Jen MacQuarrie
- Jen Mc Donough
- Jenifer Ebeling
- Jenifer Swanson

- Jenni Lynne
- Jennifer Thompson
- Jenny Fenig
- Jenny Stemmerman
- Jerad Spencer
- Jeremie Miller
- Jeremy DeMerchant
- Jeremy Epstein
- Jeremy Slate
- Jessica Brace
- Jessica Rhodes
- Jessica Roriguez
- Jessie Artigue
- Jessoca Ehrenworth
- Jevonnah Ellison
- Jill Clair
- Jill Davis
- Jill Fagan
- Jill McCulloch
- Jill Prescott
- Jim Akers
- Jim Judge
- Jim Mazziotti
- Jim Palmer
- JJ Conway
- JJ Guigan
- Jo Harlow
- Jo Lawrnce
- Jo Rosengreen
- Jo Turner
- Joan Pagano
- Joanne Miller
- Joanne Victoria

- Joash "Honey Badger" Walkins
- Jock Purtle
- Jodi Handrahan
- Jodie Milton
- Jodie Nevid
- Jody Maberry
- Joe Bernstein
- Joe Foley
- Joe Leavitt
- Joe Nicassio
- Joe Pardo
- Joel kessel
- Joelle Iseli
- Johannah Cole
- John Ashworth
- John Bolling
- John Hulen
- John Lee Dumas
- John Mojsa
- John Spender
- John Stollmeyer
- Jon Butt
- Jon Schumacher
- Jon Unal
- Jonathan Messinger
- Jonathan Schwartz
- Jordan Debbink
- Jordan Goodman
- Jordan Schumacher
- Joseph Bushnell
- Josh Bledshoe
- Joshua Sheffer

- Josie Coco
- Joy Passey
- Jody Harris
- Judy Helm Wright
- Judy Rodman
- Julia Foucht
- Julian Hayes II
- Julian Kaufmann
- Julianna Ricci
- Julie Brown
- Julie Jordan Scott
- Julie Schooler
- Justin krane
- Justin Schenk
- Kamala Chambers
- Kandis Webb
- Kara Deringer
- Karen Anderson
- Karen Dimmick
- Karen Magill
- Karen Rowe
- Karenina Jahnigen
- Karin Ovari
- Karma Senge
- Karolina Gutowski
- Kary Oberbrunner
- Kasha Slavner
- Kat Halushka
- Kate Kazony
- Kate McCarthy
- Kate Riley
- Kate Stalter
- Kather Gruver

- Katherine Kanaaneh
- Katherine Kemp Guylay
- Kathleen Gage
- Kathy Bigelow
- Katie Christy
- Katie Nall
- Katie Tassone
- Katya Livestream
- Kay Kukoyi
- Kay Newton
- Keenya Kelly
- Keita Demming
- Keith Blakemore-Noble
- Keith Norris
- Kella Price
- Kelly Cox
- Kelly Oldershaw
- Kelly Roach
- Kelly Tsagournos
- Kent Julian
- Keren Natalia
- Kevin Judge
- Kevin Young
- Khuram Malik
- Kiana Wilson
- Kiara O'Leary
- Kieron Sweeney
- Kim Smith
- Kim Sutton
- Kim Svoboda
- Kimarie
- Kimberly Adams
- Kingsley Grant

- Kirsten Anderson
- Kirsten Blake
- Kirsty Salisbury
- Knifie Burks
- Koy McDermott
- Krista Rizzo
- Kristen Darcy
- Kristi Arno
- Kristin Lloyd-Moussa
- Kristyn Tobey
- Krystle Jenna Dookoo
- Kwan Fung
- Kyle Benson
- Kyle Wagner
- Kylie Ansett
- Lane Ethridge
- Lashai Ben Salmi
- Lateefah Wielenga
- Laura Bazant
- Laura Gallagher
- Laura Lane
- Laura McGregor
- Laura Petersen
- Laura Wallace
- Lauren Lola
- Laurence O'Bryan
- Lea Ann Mallett
- Leah Notarianni
- Lee Cockerell
- Leigh Martinuzzi
- Leneic Lavalle
- Leo Knepper
- Lesley Pyne

- Lesley Yadon
- Lesslie Hassler
- Levensky Toussaint
- Lianna George
- Lila Gonzalez
- Lin Morel
- Linda Tighe
- Lindsey Anderson
- Lindsey Germono
- Line Brunet
- Lisa Ambrosch
- Lisa Brathwaite
- Lisa Crisalle
- Lisa Dadd
- Lisa Manyon
- Lisa Marie Pepe
- Lisa Marie Platske
- Lisa Pepper-Satkin
- Lisa Picou
- Lisa Sparks
- Lise Gaudreault
- Livia Pewtress
- Liz Corson Saunders
- Liz Powell
- Liz Rutledge
- Lori J. Isenstadt
- Lorna Scott
- Lorraine Tillbury
- Louie La Vella
- Louise Alerfors
- Louise Crooks
- Lucas Barra
- Lucas Mattiello

- Lucas Robak
- Lucie B Linder
- Lucy Yaldezlan
- Luis Congdon
- Luke Donovan
- Luke Scott
- Lydia Taggart
- Lyn-Dee Eldridge
- Lyndsay Phillips
- Lynn Adams
- Lynn DeBuhr Johnson
- Lynn Thier
- Mackenzly Cox
- Madelyn Victoria
- Madison Black
- Makesi Paul
- Maleeka Holawau
- Manjiri Nadkarni
- Marc Angelo Coppola
- Marc Fivecard
- Marc Mawhinney
- Marcie Peters
- Margaret Schlacter
- Margarita Millere
- Maria Horstman
- Marilyn Gordon
- Marina Marsden
- Marina Pearson
- Marissa Levin
- Mark Asquith
- Mark Duncan
- Mark Haffner
- Mark Hardcastle

- Mark Jamnik
- Mark LaMaster
- Mark LePage
- Mark Minard
- Mark Sears
- Mark Walker
- Marshall Morris
- Mary Kelly
- Mary Magpanthay
- Mary Meston
- Mary Valloni
- Mathew Passy
- Matt Fortnow
- Matt Gersper
- Matt Mauer
- Matt Miller
- Matt Mundt
- Matthew Fitzgerald
- Matthew Helderman
- Matthew Rehm
- Maureen Garry
- Maxwell Ivey
- Meg Wannkauf
- Meghan Alonso
- Mel Keyes
- Mel Sherwood
- Melanie Benson
- Melanie Mackie
- Melissa Dawn
- Melissa Gang
- Melissa Smith
- Mell Balment
- Melvin Waller

- Meridith Powell
- Michael Babcock
- Michael Blaes
- Michael Carbone
- Michael Cavitt
- Michael Cinquino
- Michael Ivanov
- Michael J. Ringer
- Michael Kass
- Michael Kawula
- Michael McGreevy
- Michael Obrien
- Michael Pasha
- Michael Prywes
- Michal Sta
- Michala Leyland
- Michele Gragnano
  Spiezia
- Michele Stanford
- Michele Stans
- Michelle Duncan-
  Wilson
- Michelle James
- Michelle Lewis
- Michelle Nagel
- Michelle Nedelec
- Michelle Norris
- Michelle Swaney
- Miguel A de Jesus
- Mike Flynn
- Mikhael Star
- Millie Leung
- Mimi Emanuel

- Mimi Lee
- Mimika Cooney
- Mindy Gibbins-Klein
- Miqael Persson
- Misty Gilbert
- Mobafa Baker
- Molly Wentzel
- Monaica Ledell
- Monica Karst
- Morgana Rae
- Myhriah Young
- Nadine Nelen
- Naomi Fox
- Natalia Dewiyani
- Nathalie Duporteau
- Nathan Clair
- Nathan Hirsch
- Neil Bartlett
- Neil Sattin
- Niccie Kliegel
- Nicholas Snapp
- Nick Loper
- Nick Pavlidis
- Nick Sonnenberg
- Nico Mellet
- Nicola Cairncross
- Nicolas Brenner
- Nicole Jansen
- Nicole Jensen
- Nicole Swiner
- Nicole Zagman
- Nicolya Williams
- Nina Amir

- Nina Babel
- Nisla Love
- Norma Waye
- Odaz (Dazzy) Lightbourne-Beneby
- Oleg Volkov
- Olivia Lewis
- Omkari Williams
- Omozua Isiramen
- Osaro Harriott
- Otakara Klettke
- P.J
- Pace Smith
- Paco Maldonado
- Pam Bayne
- Pam Masters
- Pamela Burke
- Paolo Ben Salmi
- Pat Armitstead
- Pat Duckworth
- Pat Roque
- Patricia LeBlanc
- Patrick Powers
- Patryk Wezowski
- Patty DeDominic
- Paul Brodie
- Paul Churchill
- Paul Nadeau
- Paul Rogers
- Paula Gregorowicz
- Paula Slater
- Pauline Crawford
- Peggy Galdamez
- Peggy Hallisy
- Perdita Chivers
- Peter Easling
- Peter Hhug
- Peter Radcliffe
- Petra Monaco
- Phil Gerbyshak
- Phil Klutts
- Phillip Matthew
- Phillip Scabrough
- PJ Morgan
- Pol Cousineau
- Polina Solda
- Pratima Aravabhoomi
- Prudence Monepenny
- Rachel Grant
- Rachel McGehee
- Rachel Meisels
- Rachna Jain
- Rafi Chowdhury
- Raignor Rollocks
- Randal Wark
- Raoui Anderson
- Rebecca Clayo Cloud
- Regina Huber
- Rene Brent
- Rene Brown
- Renee Vidor
- Rhiannon Rees
- Rhoberta Shaler
- Rhonda Boyle
- Rhonda McEwen
- Rhonda Smith
- Richard Liebespach
- Richard Lynch
- Richard Scott
- Richie Norton
- Rick Clemons
- Rick Fortier
- Rick Gabrielly
- Rob Dial
- Rob Farquhar
- Rob Kornblum
- Rob Walch
- Robert Rice
- Robert Szmigiel
- Robert Thibodeau
- Robin Bates
- Robyn Torre
- Rod Janz
- Roddy Maciver
- Rodney Turner
- Rohan Chaubey
- Ron Myers
- Ron Tester
- Ron Tsang
- Rondel Benjamin
- Rosemary Heenan
- Roxanne St. Clair
- Rusty Pang
- Ruthie Slingerland
- Ryan Ramoutar
- Ryan Stewman
- S.T Wilkinson
- Sabah Ali
- Sabrina Ben Salimi

- Sabrina Redmond
- Sandi Amorim
- Sarah Cameron
- Sarah Jane Ponce
- Sarah Kravitz
- Sarah Li Cain
- Sarah Santacroce
- Sarah Williams
- Sasha Niala
- Scot Perkins
- Scott Allan
- Scott Eddy
- Scott Paton
- Scott Roberts
- Sean Douglas
- Sean Richardson
- Seema Alexander
- Serena Star Leonard
- Sergio Livingston
- Seth Benham
- Shane DeGaray
- Shane Krider
- Shane Scott
- Sharon Bowe
- Shawn Chambers
- Shawn McBride
- Shea Wingler
- Sheila Sutherland
- Sheila Unique
- Shelsey Jarvis
- Sherell Brown
- Sherna Alexander
- Sherry Savage

- Shirley Gutkowski
- Shonda Holt
- Simon Jordan
- Simone Vincenzi
- Skip Weisman
- Sondra Kornblatt
- Sophia Bera
- Sophie Bailey
- Stacy Tuschl
- Stephanie Andrews
- Stephanie Calahan
- Stephanie George
- Stephanie McAuliffe
- Stephanie O'Dea
- Stephen Hobbs
- Stephen Scoggins
- Steve Cunningham
- Steve Olsher
- Steve Rodgers
- Steven Haggerty
- Steven R. McEvoy
- Stuart Knight
- Stuart Woodrow
- Sue Gulher
- Sully Ali
- Summer Weirich
- Sunni Dawson
- Sunny Johnston
- Susan Barber
- Susan Davis
- Susan Hasty
- Susan Heaton Wright
- Susanna Halonene

- Susanna Utbult
- Susheela Ramachandra
- Suzanne Young
- Suzi Parkus
- Svava Brooks
- T. Allen Hanes
- Tahir Hussain
- Tahira Amar Khan
- Tahsha Hollister
- Tamba Gwindi
- Tameka Anderson
- Tammi Durden
- Tammie Pike
- Tammy Hudgin
- Tamsin Young
- Tandee Salter
- Tandy Gutierrez
- Tania Vasallo
- Tanisha Layne
- Tanisha Williams
- Tanner The Great Gears
- Tanya Destang
- Tanya Lynn Thomas
- Tanya Rineer
- Tara Alemany
- Tara Murulli
- Tema Frank
- Teresa Blaes
- Teresa de Grosbois
- Teresa Kuhn
- Terry Dika Volchoff
- Terry Green
- Terry Lancaster

Y.O.U.R.S.
Your Own Unique Real Self

- Terry Maxwell
- Terry Stafford
- Terry Wildemann
- Terryn Barill
- Tess Vergara
- Thembi Baker
- Theresa Obeirne
- Thom Singer
- Thor Conklin
- Tim Matthew
- Tim Melanson
- Tim Paige
- Tina Dietz
- Tina Herring
- Tinesha Cherry
- Tisa Yont
- Todd Malloy
- Tom Corley
- Tom Dowd
- Tom Matzen
- Tom Morkes
- Tom Schwab
- Tomi Grover
- Tommy Baker
- Tony J Selimi
- Tony St.Clair
- Tony Winyard
- Tonya Farrens
- Torie Robinson
- Tracey Minutolo
- Tracy Clark
- Travis Collier
- Tray-Sean Ben Salmi
- Trish Cardona
- Trista Ainsworth
- Tyler Basu
- Umar Tariq
- Uttam Maraz
- Valerie Sheppard
- Valerie Young
- Vanessa Cabrera
- Vanessa Gaboleiro
- Vanessa Jackson
- Vanessa Moraes
- Vange Dardouni
- Vartika Manasvi
- Veenu Keller
- Vergel Alvarez
- Veronica Grant
- Veronica Jones
- Veronica Kirin
- Veronica Ray
- Vicky Farquhar
- Victoria Bolton
- Vidal Cisneros
- Vidya Ravi
- Vikki Parker
- Vincent Pugliese
- Vinnie Tortorich
- Virginia Jimenez
- Virginia Phillips
- Virginia Ritter busch
- Vit Singh
- Viveka Von Rosen
- Wade Mark
- Wael Badawe
- Wally Carmichael
- Walt & Egypt Charles
- Warren Nye
- Warren Pole
- Wayne Herring
- Wendy Dewar Hughes
- Wendy Harrison
- Wendy McClelland
- Wendy Williams
- Wendy Yost
- Wes Ferguson
- Will Aylward
- Willow Green
- Yanique Grant
- Yann ilunga
- Yannick Jacob
- Yara Kanaaneh
- Yasmine Ben Salmi
- Yengyee Lor-Yang
- Yoram Solomon
- Yuri Elkaim
- Yuri Kruman
- Yvonne Garris
- Zach Benson
- Zach Loeb
- Zee Martin
- Zev Asch
- Zoe Mckey

My #12minconvos continue and can be listened everyday at:
www.twelveminuteconvos.com

twelveminuteconvos.com

Printed in Great Britain
by Amazon